Sports

Elizabeth Nonweiler

raintree

silat

ping pong

pool

sledding

zorbing

rafting

sprinting

money
42658
adidas
Virgin money
9383
adidas
9187
GILES
fighting
motor
neurone
disease
Virgin money
9488
adidas

marathon

ballooning

aquatics

snorkelling

acrobatics

Interesting facts about the pictures

page 2: **Silat** is a martial art. Silat students practise staying still and balancing, precise footwork and how to defend themselves and stop a fight. They are taught to be polite and respectful towards others.

page 3: **Ping pong** is sometimes called table tennis. The players hit a ball back and forth on a hard table with a racket. They have to move fast to hit the ball back before it bounces twice on their side.

page 4: **Pool** is played on a special table with six pockets round the sides. There are heavy coloured balls on the table. The player tries to hit a ball with a stick called a cue to make the balls roll into the pockets.

page 5: **Sledding** takes place outside in the snow on something that will slide easily called a sled. The rider pulls the sled up a slope, sits or lies on it and zooms down. If the snow is icy, the sled moves very fast.

page 6: **Zorbing** means rolling down a gentle slope inside a ball made of transparent plastic called a zorb. A rider can be strapped in a zorb or left free to walk or to be tossed around. The boy in this zorb is walking.

page 7: **Rafting** takes place in an inflatable raft on a river with rough water running over rocks. It is exciting, but it can be dangerous, so the people in the picture are wearing hard hats and life jackets in case they fall out.

page 8: **Sprinting** means running at top speed over a short distance. This runner is competing in a race, running on a track. The fastest runners in the world can run 100 metres in about 10 seconds.

page 9: A **marathon** is a run for about 42 kilometres. The runners must move more slowly, so that they have enough energy to keep going. This is a picture of people running a marathon along a road in London.

page 10: **Ballooning** involves getting in a basket hanging below a balloon. A burner above the basket heats the air in the balloon, the hot air rises and the balloon goes up into the sky and is carried along by the wind.

page 11: **Aquatics** are water sports, like the synchronised swimming in this picture. The swimmers have to be good at swimming, acrobatics, dance, precise timing and holding their breath, even when they are upside down.

page 12: **Snorkelling** means swimming underwater while breathing through a tube attached to a mask. The tube goes from the swimmer's mouth to the air above the surface of the water. This boy can see fish clearly.

page 13: **Acrobatics** are extraordinary performances of gymnastics and dance. Acrobats must be strong, flexible and good at balancing. They learn how to do rolls, cartwheels and handstands safely.

Letter-sound correspondences

Level 1 books cover the following letter-sound correspondences. Letter-sound correspondences highlighted in **green** can be found in this book.

ant	big	cat	dog	egg	fish	get	hot	it
jet	key	let	man	nut	off	pan	queen	run
sun	tap	up	van	wet	box	yes	zoo	

duck	fish	chips	sing	thin this	keep	look moon	art	corn